Simple 1-2-3™

EASTER

COLOR & FRAME

new seasons®

a division of Publications International, Ltd.

Let's get social!

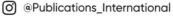

@Publications_International

@PublicationsInternational

www.pilbooks.com

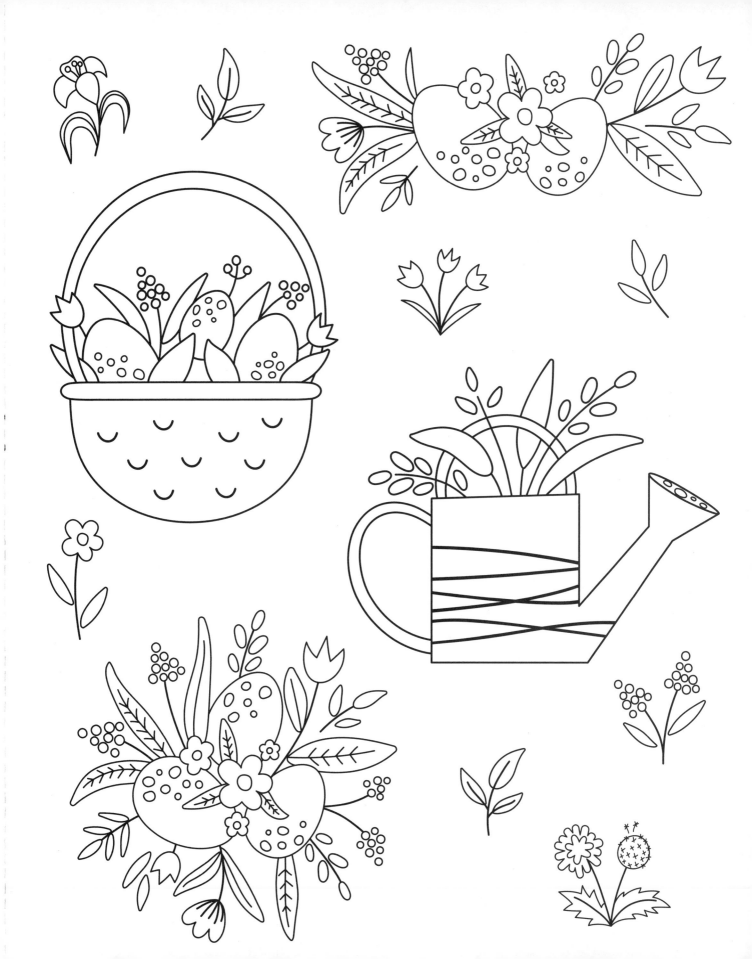

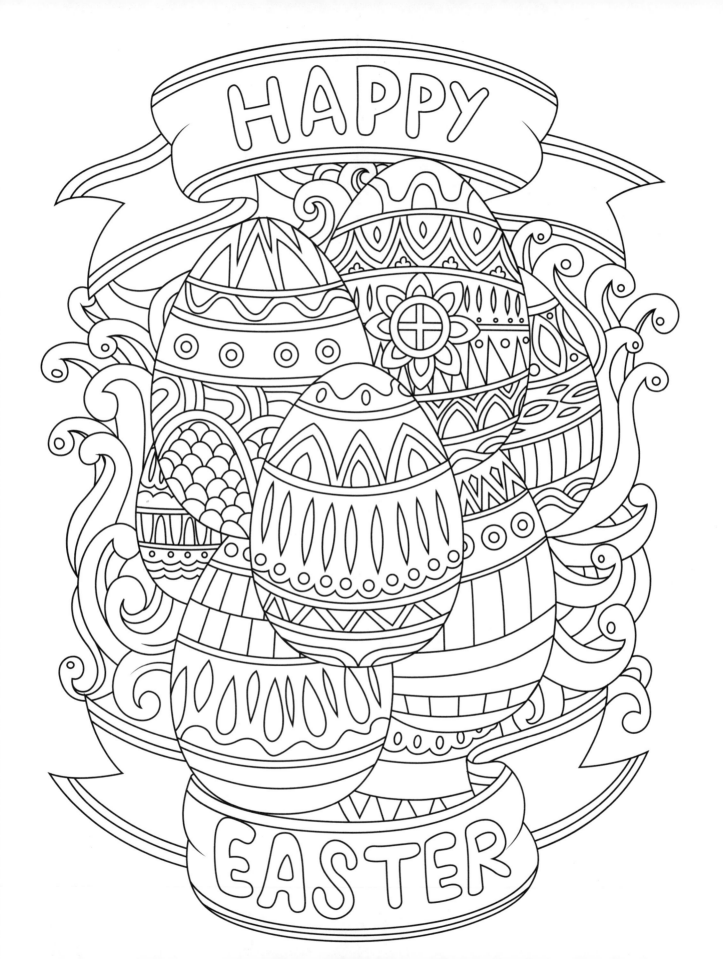

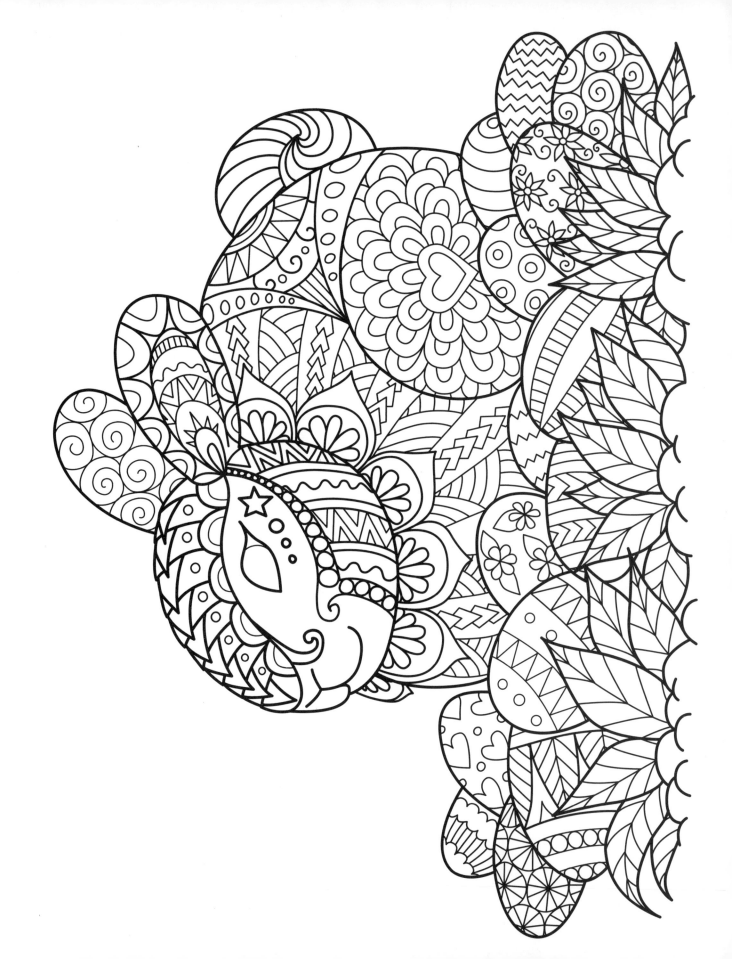

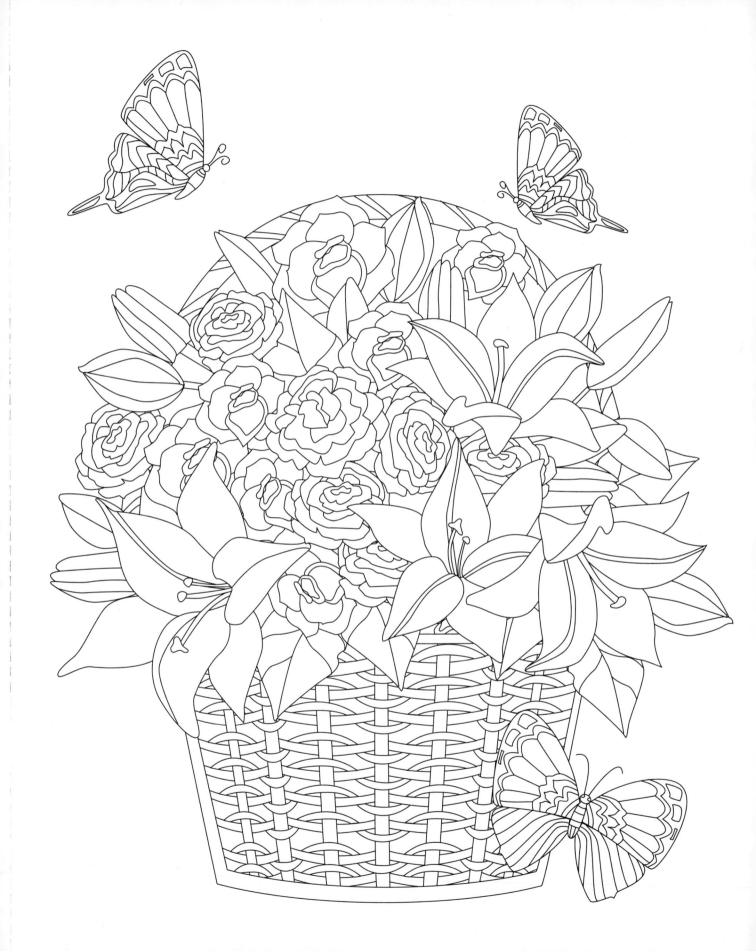

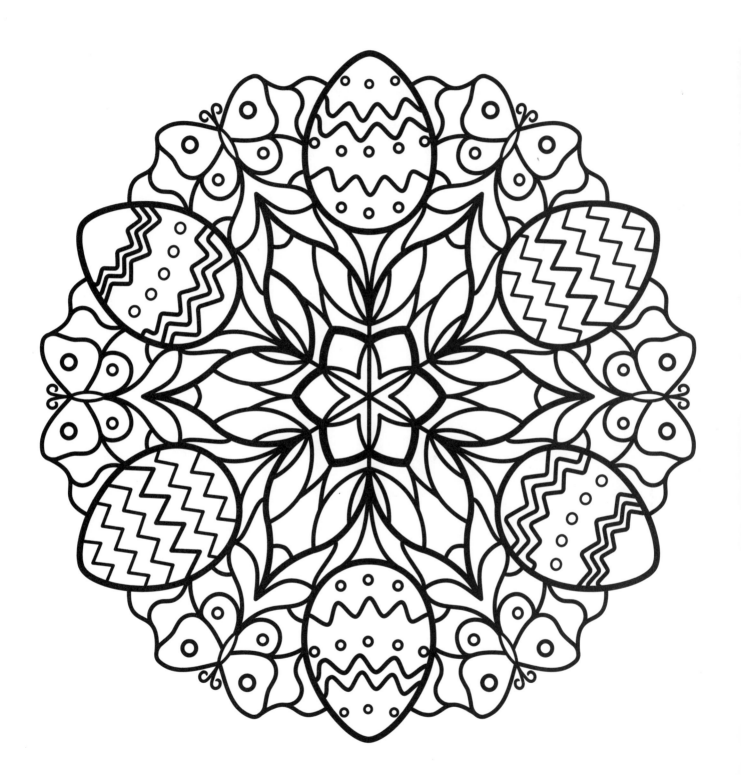

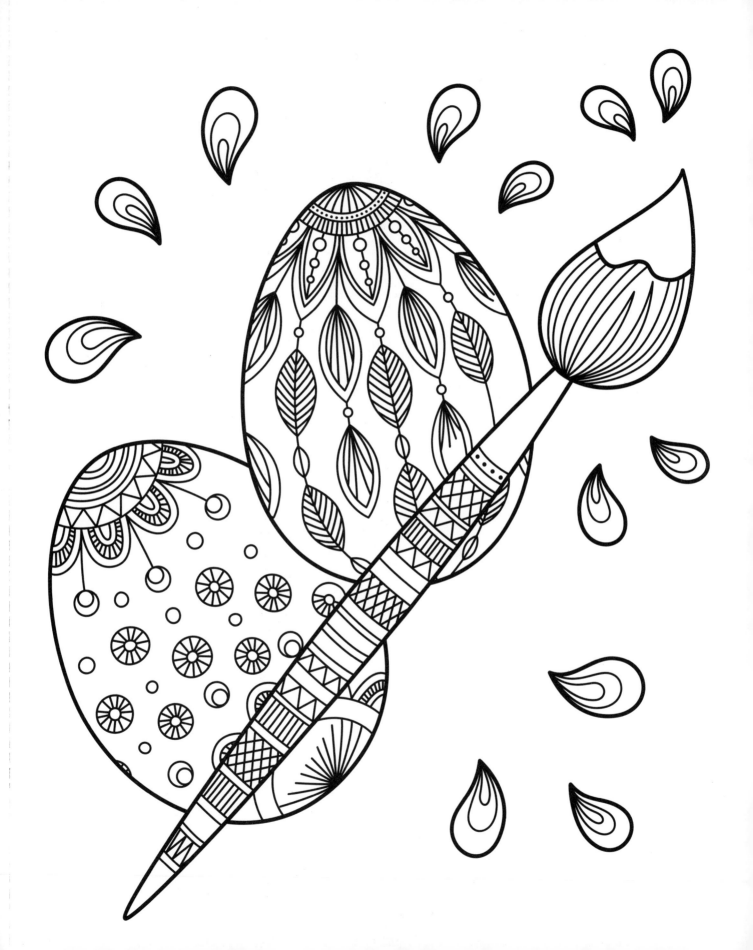

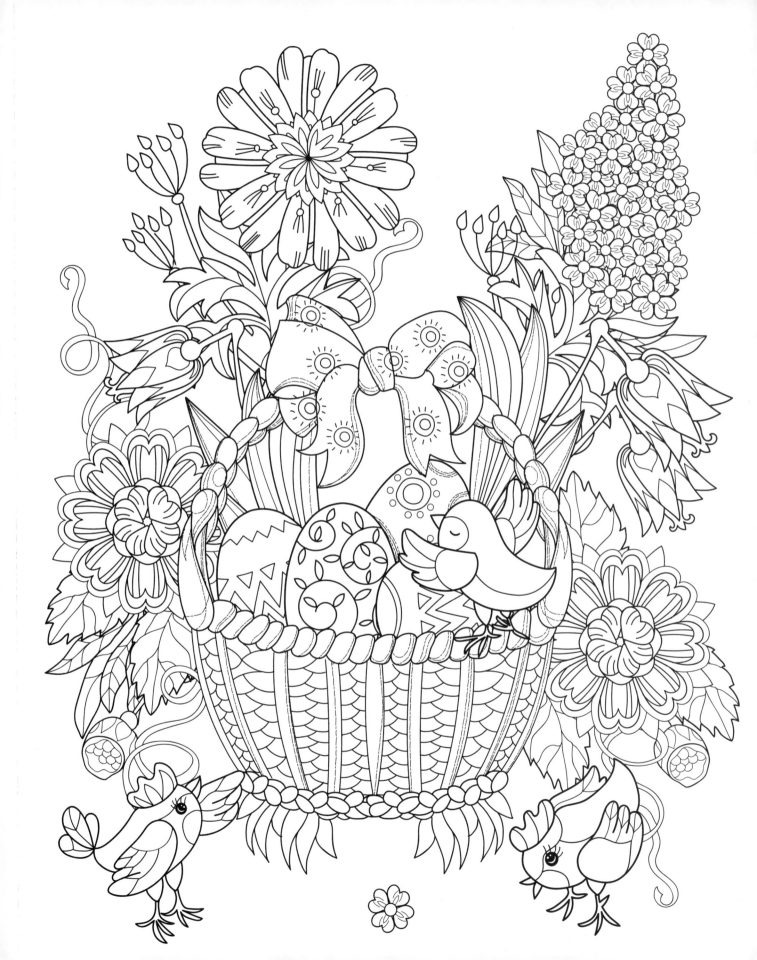

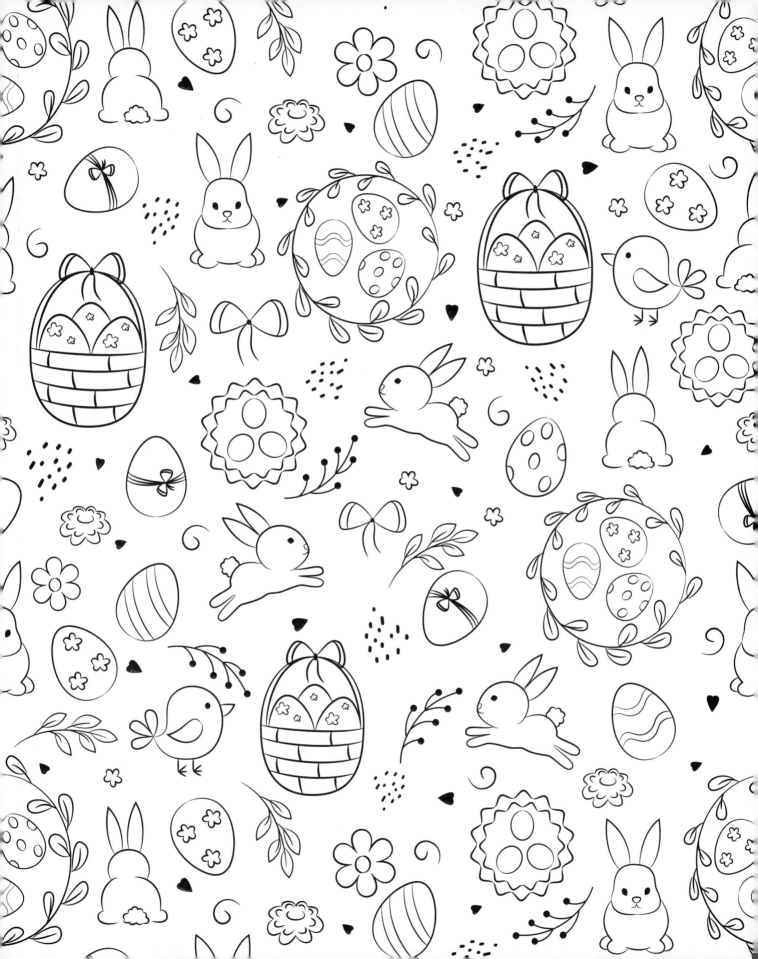

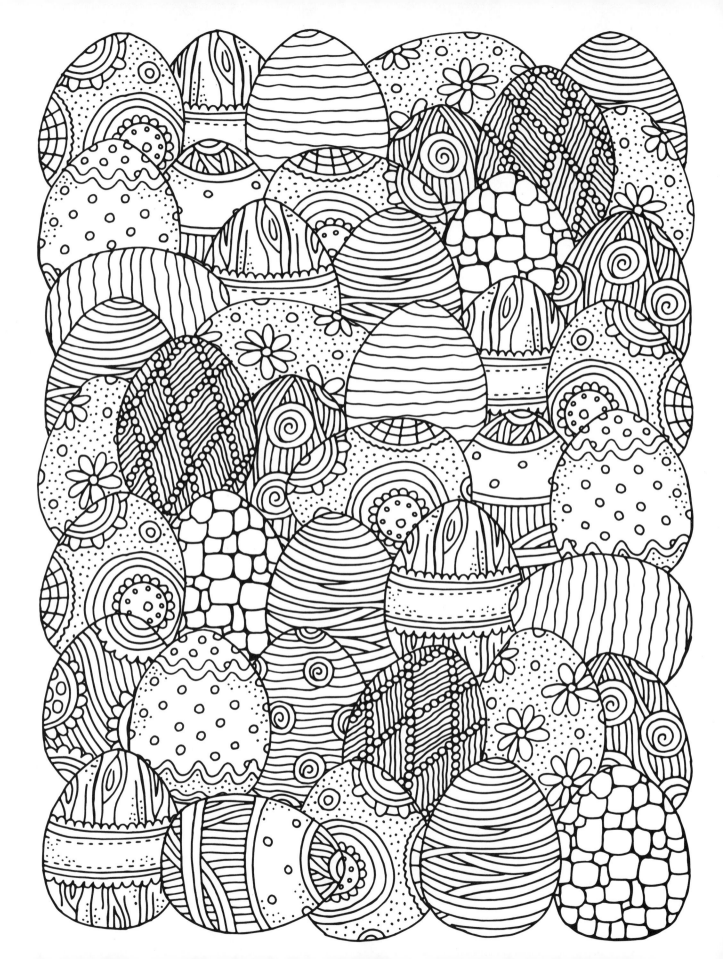

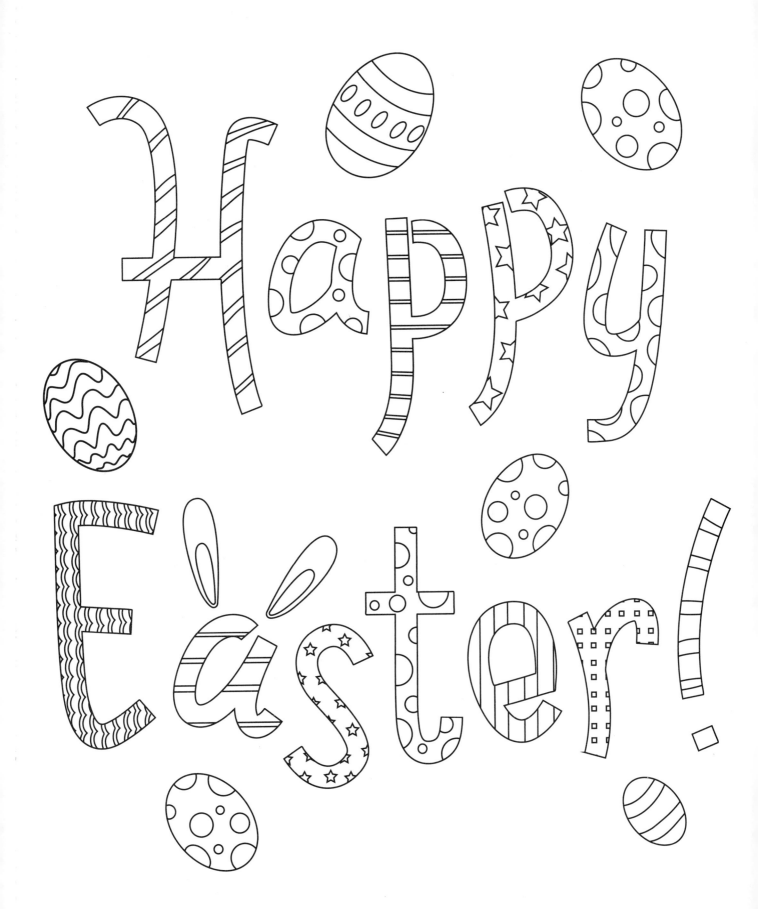

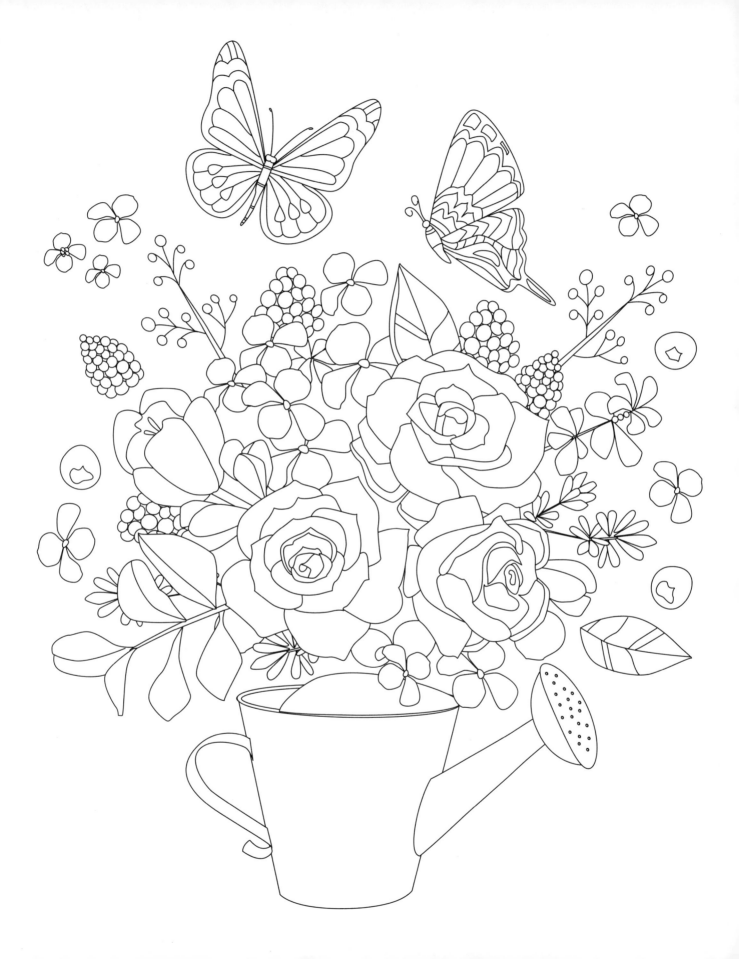

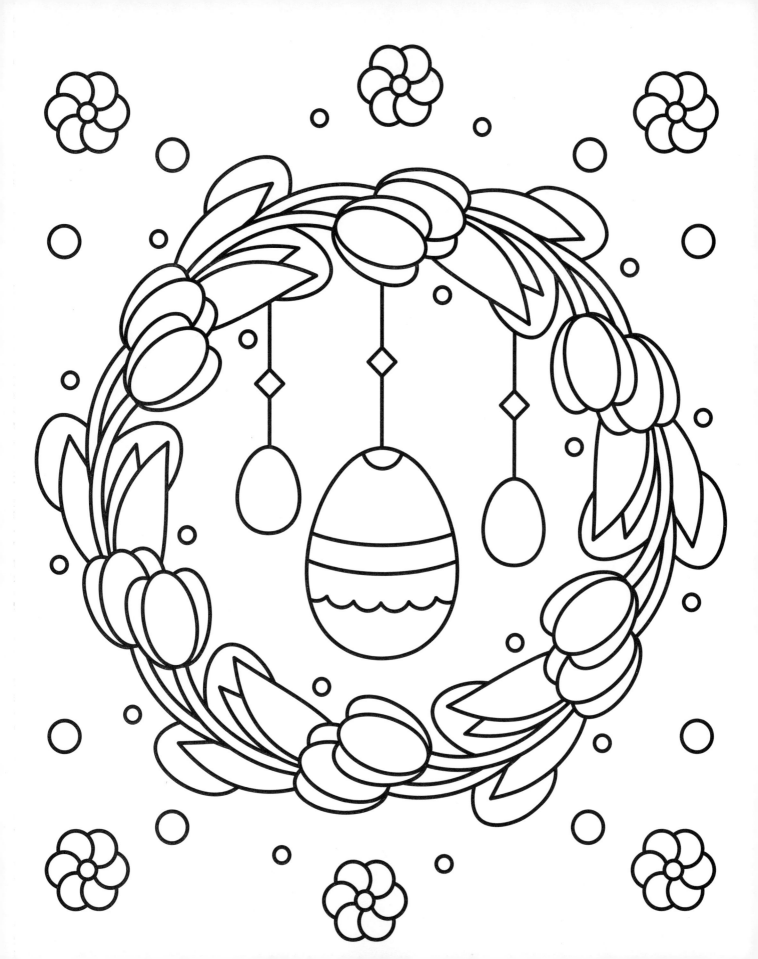

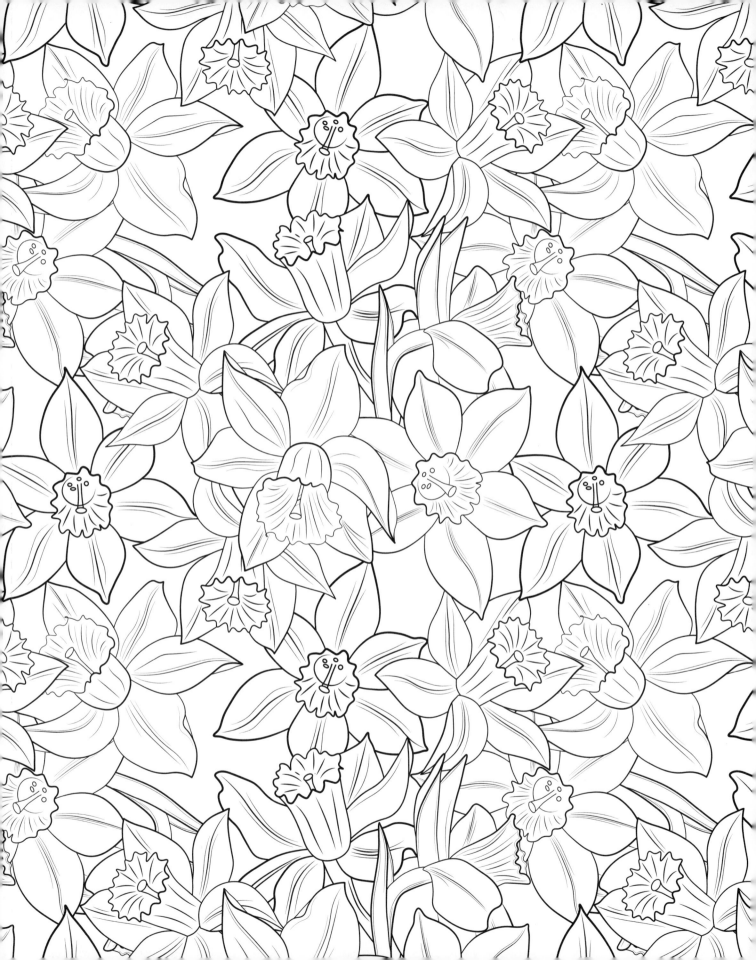

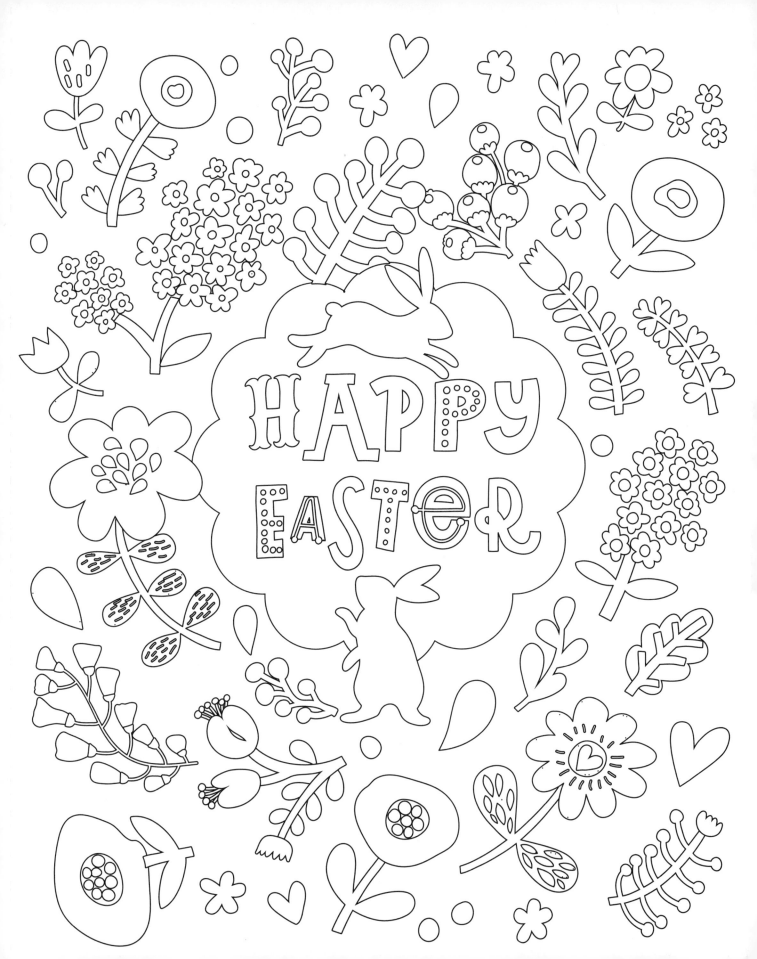

HAPPY EASTER

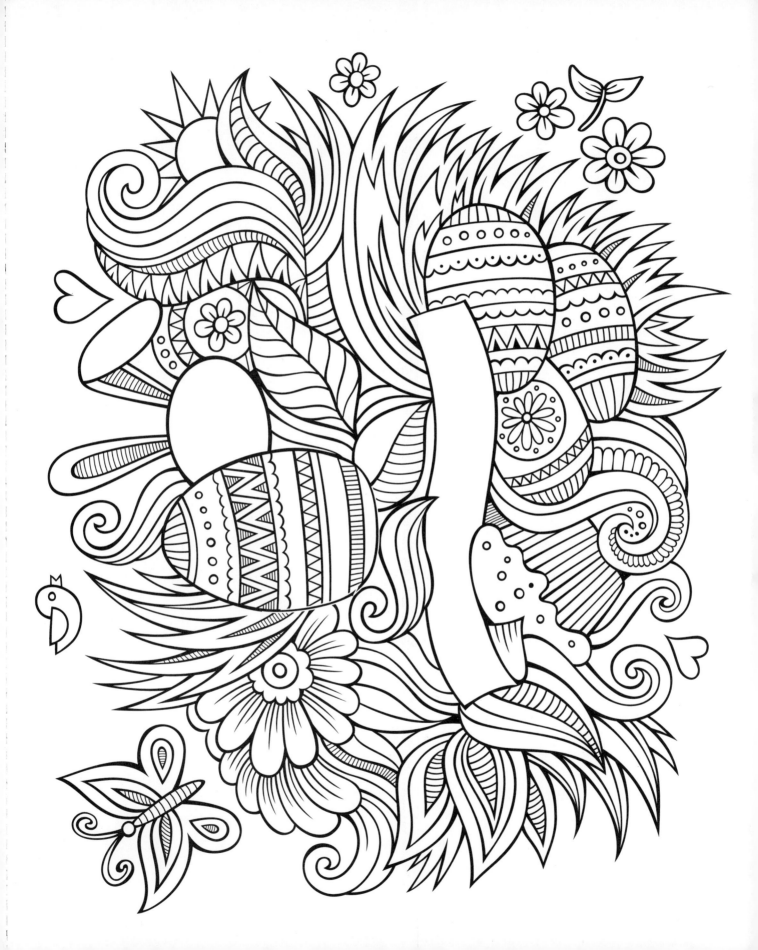

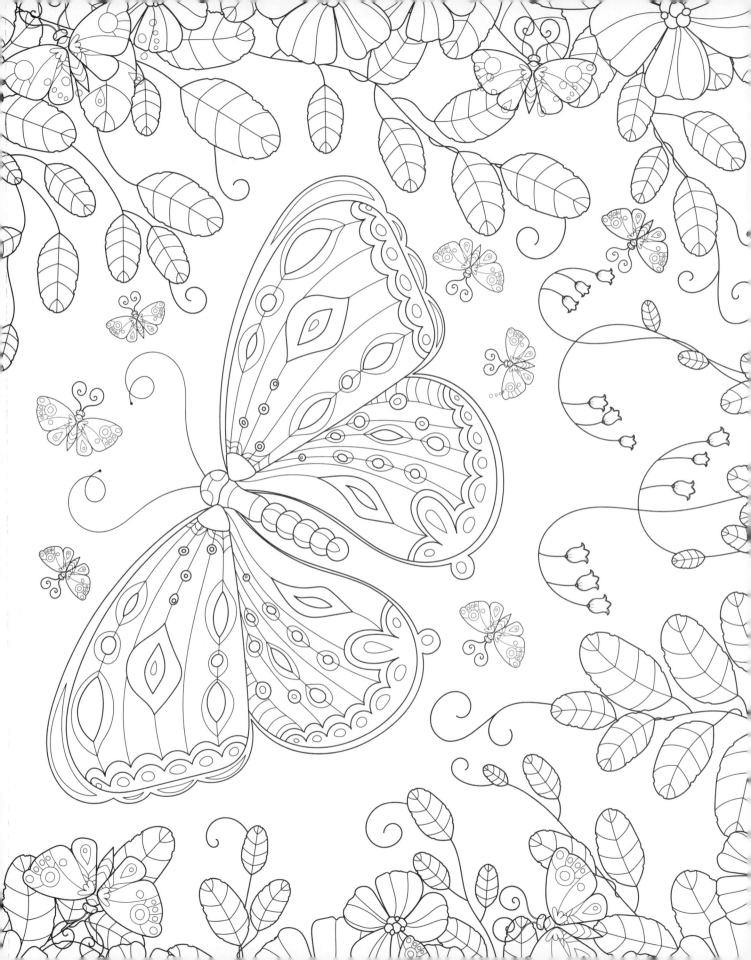

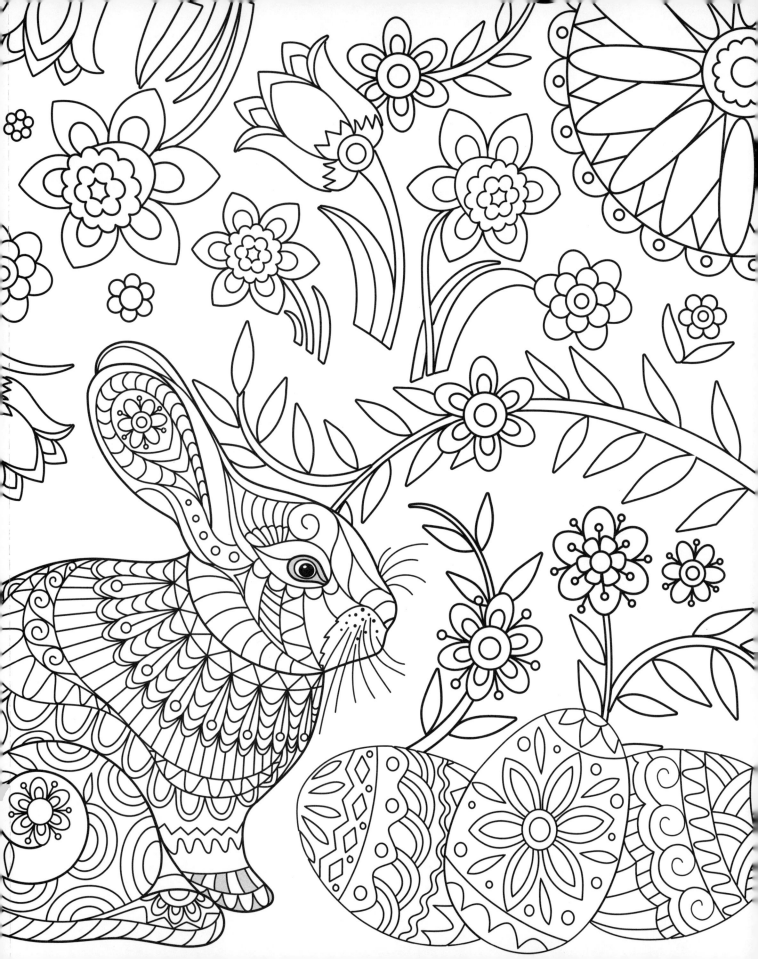

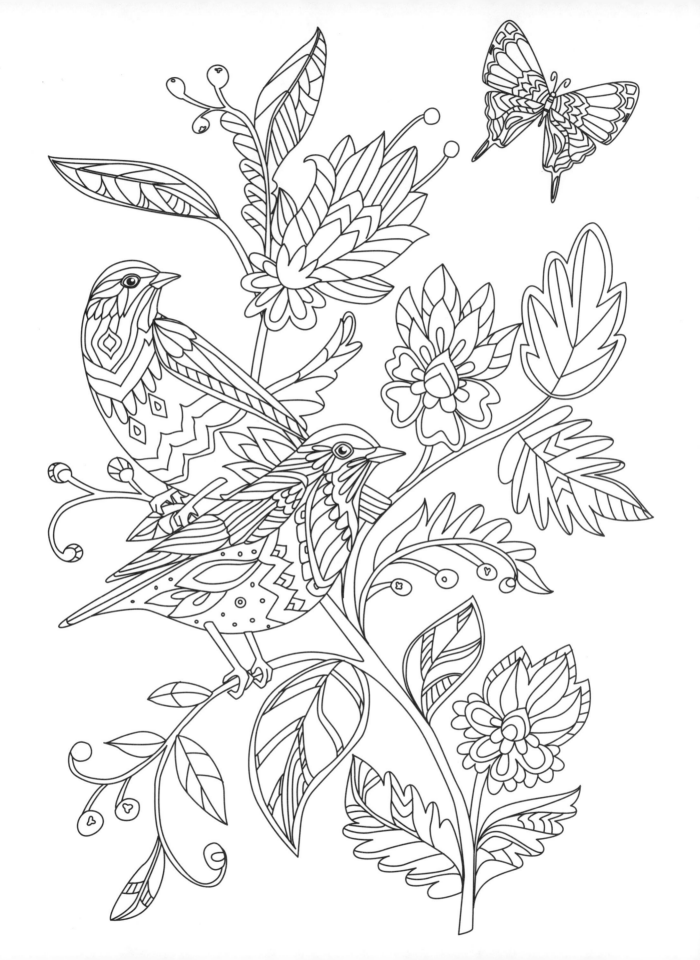

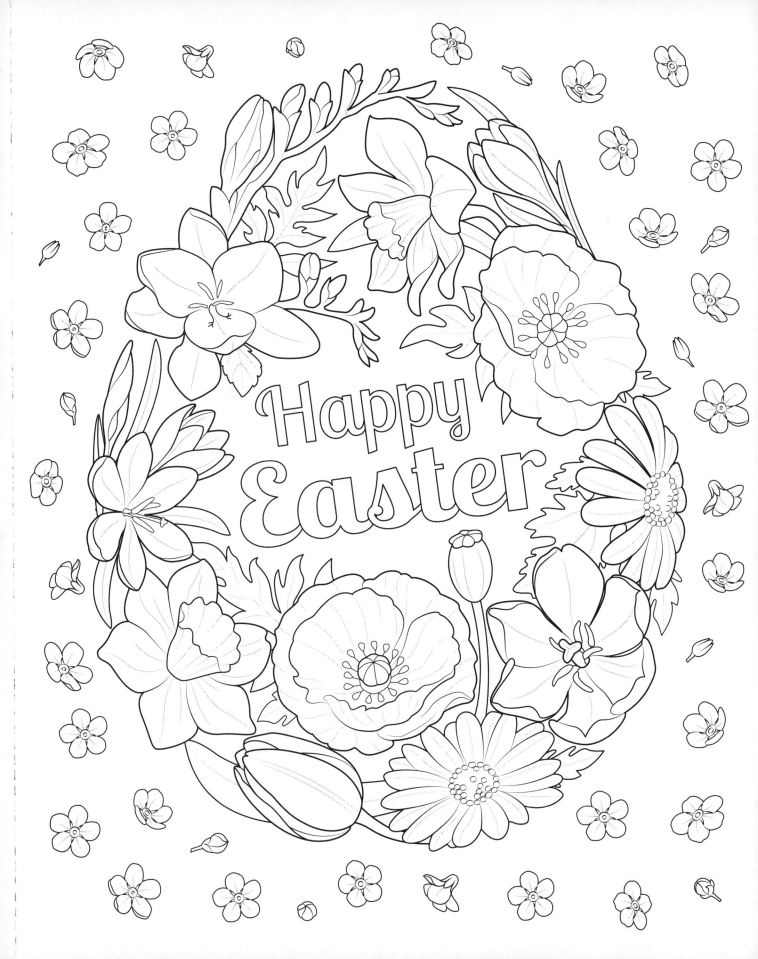

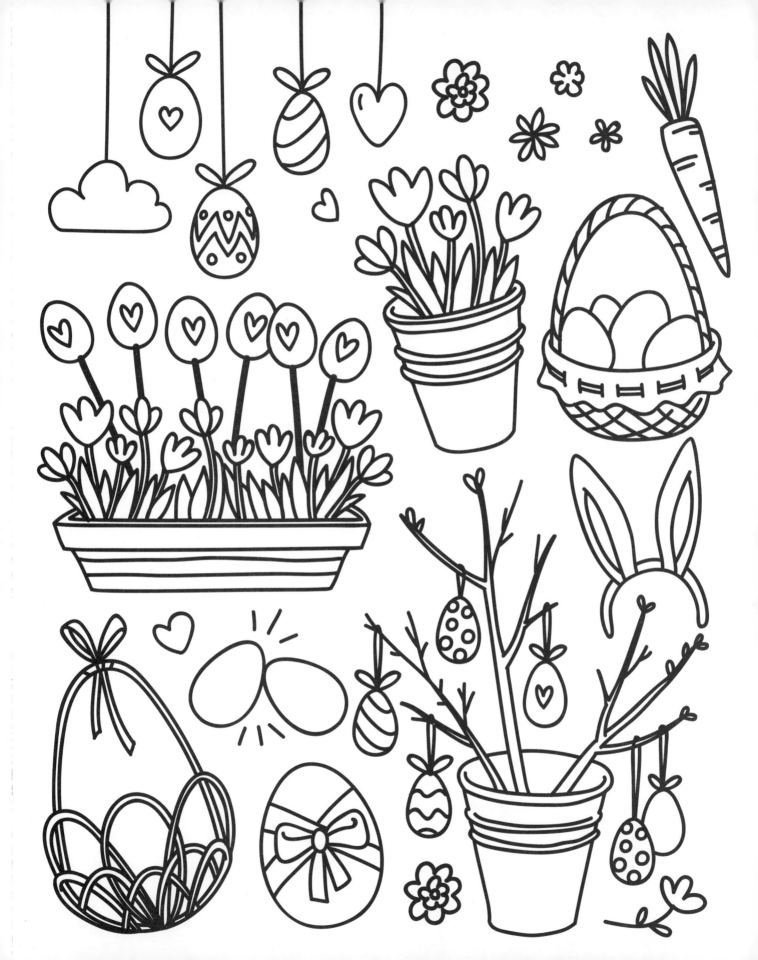

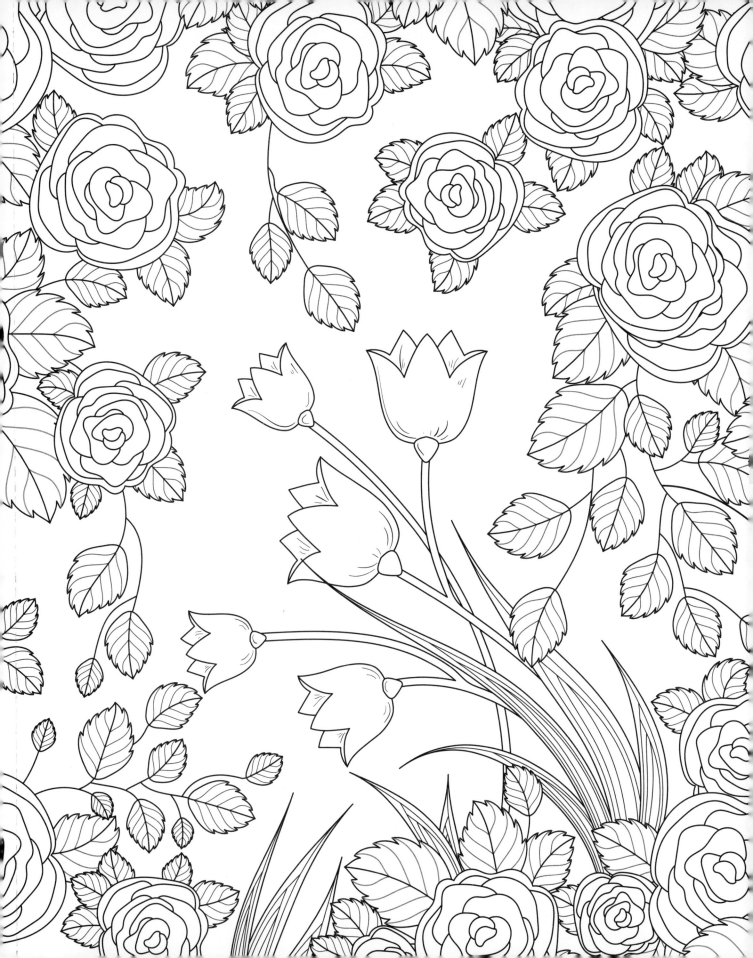

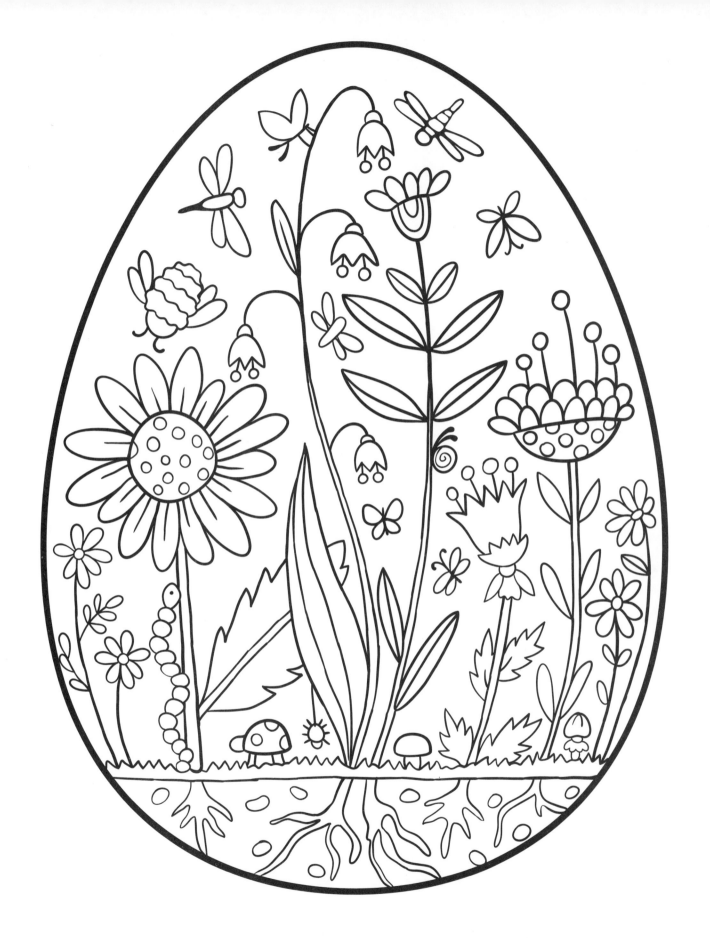

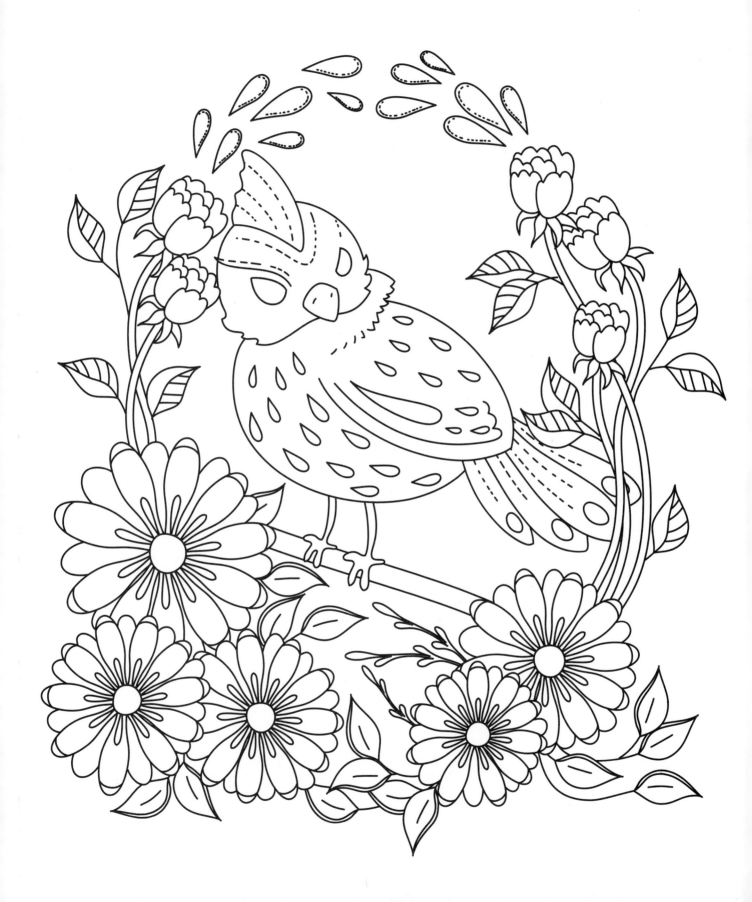

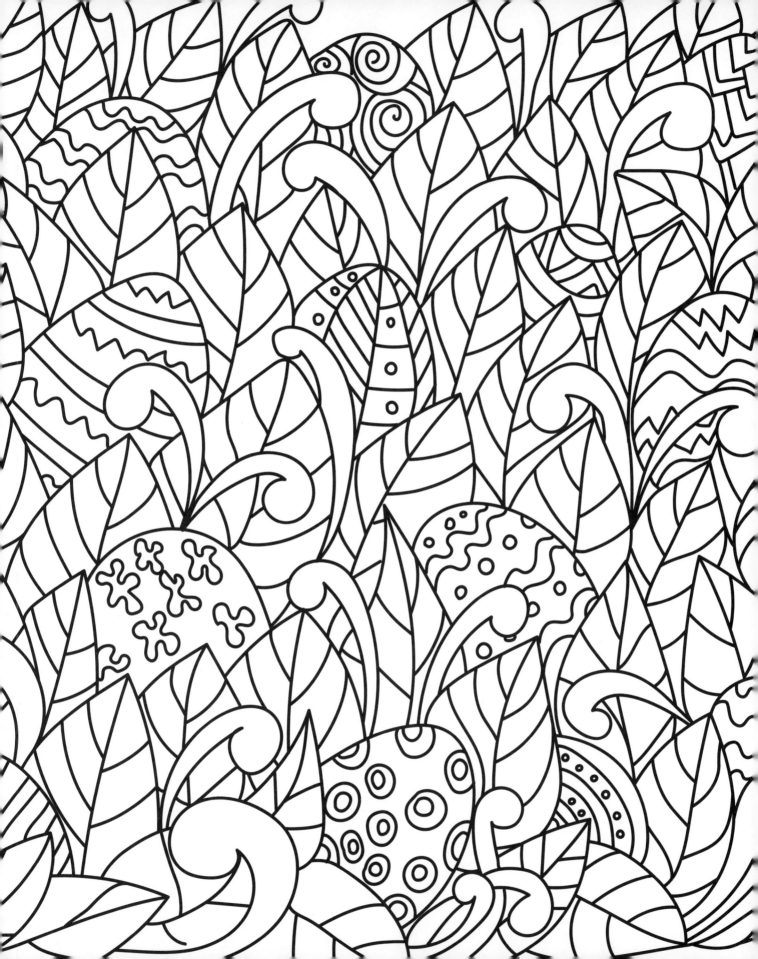

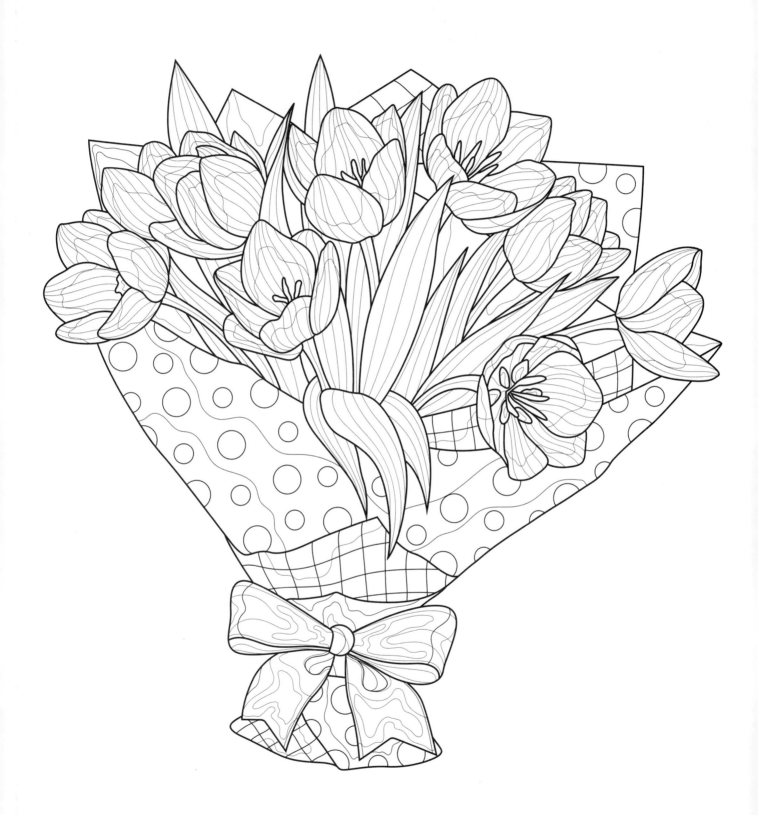

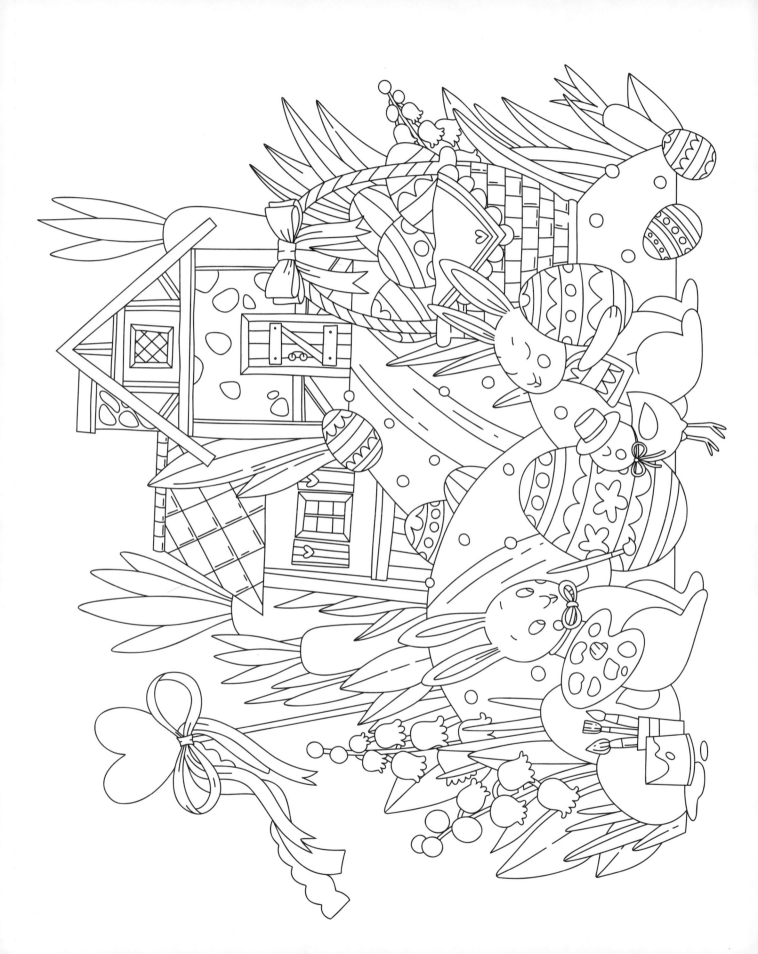

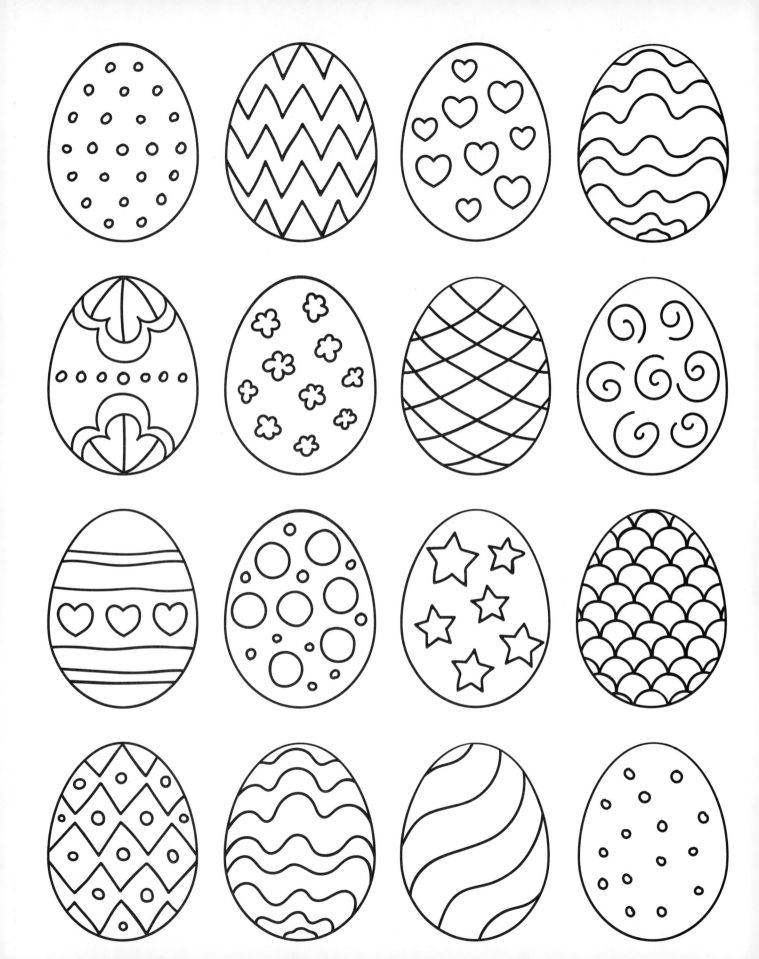

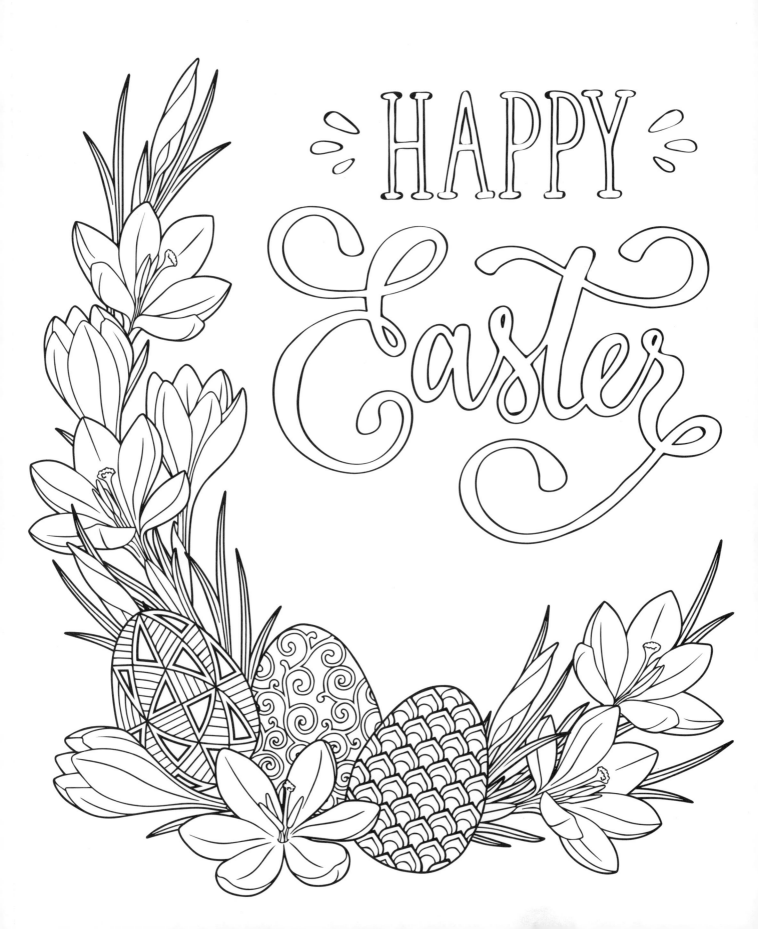

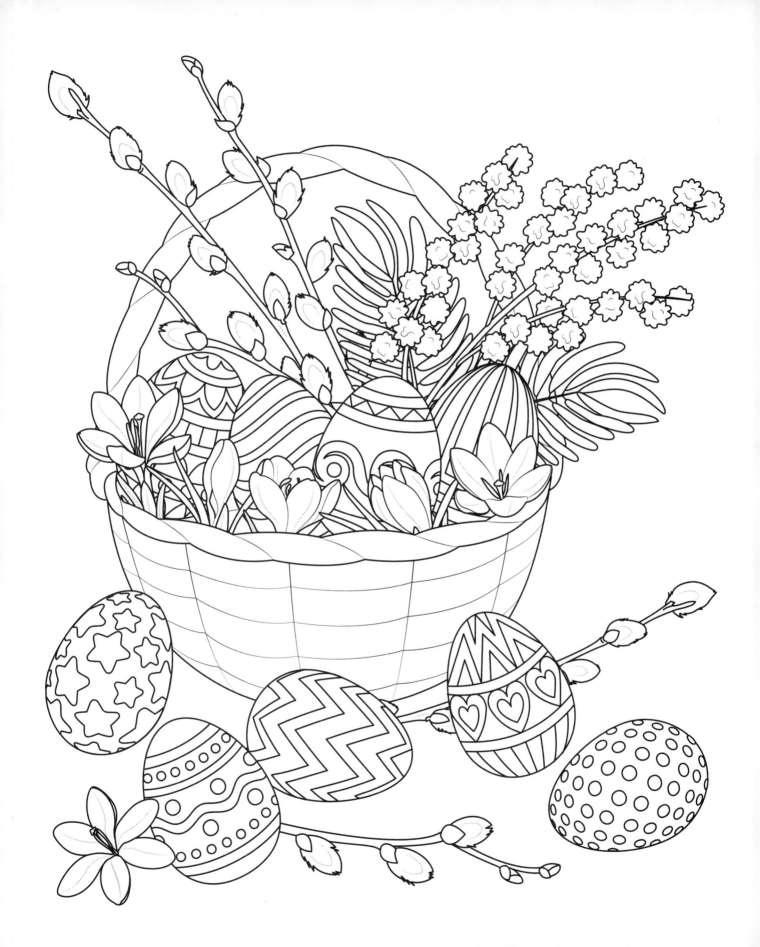

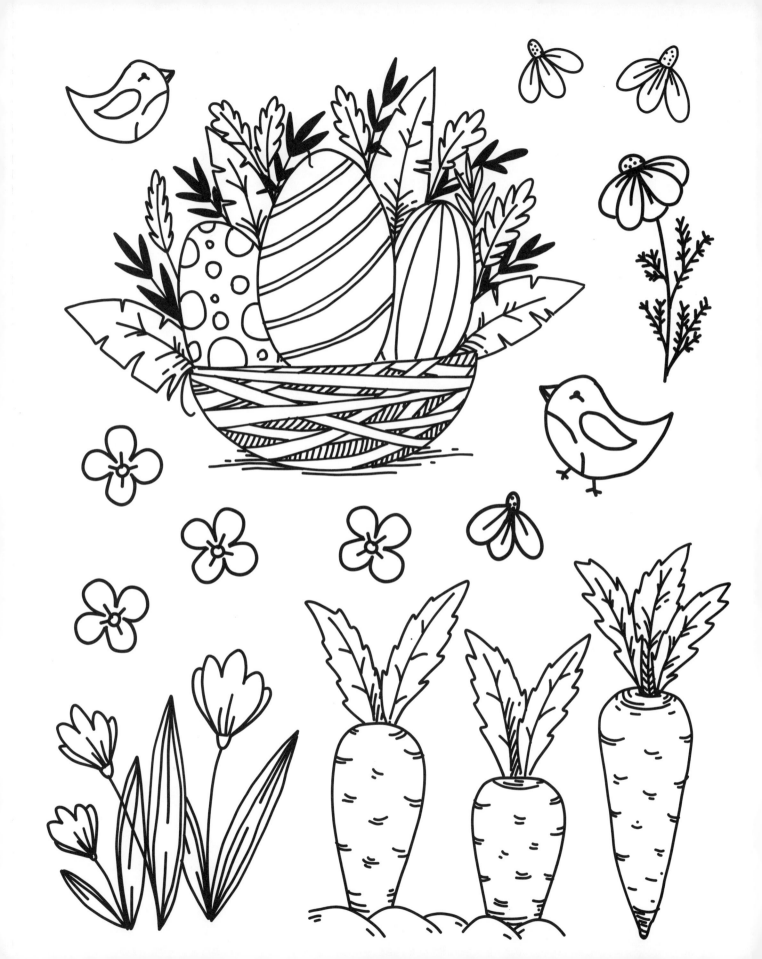